How to draw
MONSTERS

Written and Illustrated by Barry Green
Edited by Susie Hodge

First published in Great Britain by Funfax Ltd.,
an imprint of Dorling Kindersley Limited,
9 Henrietta Street, London WC2E 8PS
Funfax concept © Funfax Ltd.
Text and illustrations © 2000 Funfax Ltd.
© & TM The Media Merchants TV Co Ltd.
All rights reserved.

TOOLS AND MATERIALS

Paper
If you just want to practise your drawing skills, use cheap paper you won't mind throwing away if you don't like the results. You could use the plain back of scrap paper. If you are drawing a picture you want to keep, cartridge paper is good to use and can be bought in pads of different sizes.

Pencils
Start your drawings using a 2H or HB pencil. A 2H pencil makes hard, faint lines. It is good for planning out your picture, but the lines can be difficult to rub out if you press too hard.

Pens
Once you have your pencil drawing as you'd like it, outline it using a black fineliner pen then rub out all the pencil lines. If you are using felt-tip pens or paints to colour the picture in, it's best to use a waterproof black pen so that you won't smudge your lines.

Keep a small sketchbook and a pencil with you wherever you go, then you can draw interesting things you see – the more you draw, the better you'll become!

COLOURING IN

Coloured pencils
You can colour in your picture using coloured pencils. Start off lightly then gradually darken the colour by pressing harder.

Felt-tip pens
These are good for colouring in, especially when you want nice bright colours.

Poster paints and acrylics
These paints are great for mixing together to create new colours. Tone down their colour by adding more water or mixing in white.

TIP

A good way of colouring in is to use felt-tip pens or paints as a base, then add shading with coloured pencils.

MAKING MONSTERS

From real monsters such as giant snakes, and dinosaurs, to famous fiends, witches and ogres...there's a whole bunch of beasties for you to draw!

You can turn the most unlikely things into monsters. Look how this little mouse can be transformed!

Of course, not all monsters have to be nasty. Some can be friendly, like this little devil.

Most monsters have things in common, such as big, pointed teeth, claws and a scary expression.

Evil

Evil smile

Mad

Your monsters will look even more spooky if you put them in the right setting. Choose some of the creepy things shown below, and add them to your backgrounds.

SCARY TREE

BATS

FORK LIGHTNING

SPOOKY CASTLE

FULL MOON

HIDDEN EYES

SPOOKY SWAMP

SKULL AND BONES

COBWEB AND SPIDER

CANDLE

HOW TO DRAW MONSTERS

5

WEREWOLF

Draw this scary man-beast.

Start by drawing these simple shapes.

Add facial features and a hand, leg and foot.

Fill in the details more fully, such as the nostrils, nails and clothes.

Finish off your werewolf as shown. Finally, add a full moon. Outline and colour him in!

6

WEREWOLF'S FACE

Now draw him in close-up.

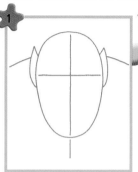

Draw an oval shape for the head, indicate ears and add a cross on the face.

Use the cross as a guide to draw the face shape and features. Draw in part of the body.

Add more facial features. Pay attention to the eyes.

Draw in the teeth, dark eyes and ears. Add hair using lots of short strokes. Finish by colouring him in.

TERRIBLE T. REX

Draw the biggest meat-eating dinosaur of them all!

Draw two ovals for the head and body. Add guides for the arms, legs and tail. Note the cross in the head oval.

Sketch the shape of the body more fully, using simple lines and shapes. Mark on the eye and mouth.

Shape the legs and put in the razor-sharp teeth!

To finish off, use rough lines to indicate dinosaur skin. Draw a background and colour it all in.

8

Try this famous three-horned plant-eater.

1

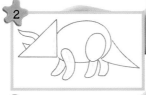

Sketch the simple shapes shown here. Draw lines for the legs and horns.

2

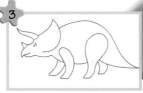

Flesh out the legs and horns.

3

Sketch in the head shape. Draw a mouth and an eye.

Add the beak-like mouth and bony frill. Use small circular shapes for skin. Outline your Triceratops and colour him in. He looks like he's ready to charge!

FIERY DRAGON

Tackle this fiendish fire-breather.

1

Draw a circle for the body and triangles for wings. Draw the head with a cross as shown, and lines for arms and legs.

2

Using simple shapes, draw in the tail, legs, ears and fingers. Notice the triangular tail tip.

3

Complete the wing shapes.

Sketch the shape of the head, eyes and flared nostrils. Draw the legs, arms and wings in more detail. Add a simple shape to show a flame.

Finish off your dragon with scales on the skin, movement lines, smoke, flames and a bit of background scenery. Just look at those prickly body spikes, fierce claws, the swishing tail and the fiery breath! Call for a knight!

SSSCARY SNAKE

Sketch a slithering reptile.

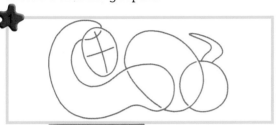

Sketch an oval for the head. Then draw a
bendy shape for the first part of the body,
an oval for the middle part and a circle for
the third part. Add the tail shape at the end.
Mark a cross on the face.

Using the cross as a guide, put in facial
features: eyes, a mouth, fangs and a tongue.

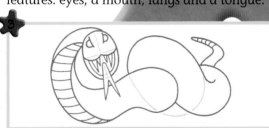

Draw in part of the body and the tail
as shown.

Draw the finishing details on the face, then add a pattern on the body. Copy the pattern here or choose your own: spots, zigzags or stripes – it's up to you. Movement lines around the tail make it look as if he's 'rattling' it.

Draw scenery around the snake. Make him look really huge by drawing miniature trees. Colour the whole picture in bold, bright colours.

GIANT SQUID

Try drawing this massive marine monster.

Draw an egg-shaped oval for the body with a diamond shape on the end. Lightly sketch where the tentacles will go.

Draw in the tentacles and the eyes.

Add a skin pattern and suckers on the tentacles.

HOW TO DRAW MONSTERS

Make your giant squid look more impressive by putting him in a sea setting. Colour the complete picture in to finish.

MONSTER SPIDER

Have a go at this awesome arachnid!

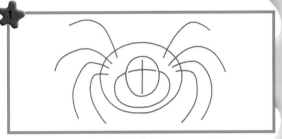

Draw a circle for the head, two ovals for the body and lines where the eight legs will go.

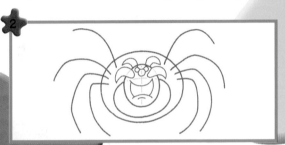

Add details to the head: three eyes, a huge mouth and fangs.

Fill in the legs.

4

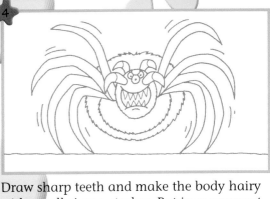

Draw sharp teeth and make the body hairy with small zigzag strokes. Put in movement lines to show the spider scuttling.

To make him seem even more monstrous, draw the spider in a city scene like this. Or make up a scene of your own. Notice how hairy this spider is – it's even on his legs! Outline your picture and colour it in.

GHOULISH GHOST

Here's a classic ghost for you to draw.

1

Draw a cross.

2

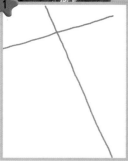

Hang a sheet on it. Add eyes and a mouth.

3

Finish by drawing extra details such as the green slime and shiver lines.

4

Using the same shapes, you can also create a friendly ghost!

Now try this headless version!

1

Draw the simple shapes as shown.

2

Lightly sketch further details such as the face, tunic and wavy, ghostly legs.

3

Add more details to the head, neck and hands.

4

Draw all the finishing touches and add a background. A brick wall is effective, as it looks as if the ghost is drifting through it!

19

SHOCKER SKULL

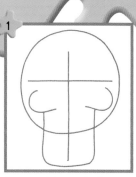

1

Start with a circle for the top of the skull. Sketch in two cheek shapes and the jaw. Add a cross to help you position the features.

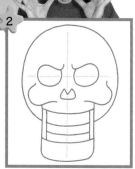

2

Sketch in the eye and nose holes and lightly draw the mouth. Notice how the bottom of the top teeth follow the line of the skull circle.

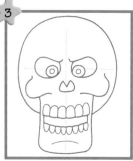

3

Draw in the eyeballs and tombstone teeth.

4

Finish off by adding cracks, cobwebs and a dangly spider to make it extra spooky.

DANCING SKELETON

Now try this demon dancer.

1

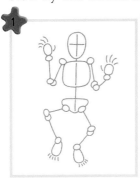

Draw an oval for the head, a rounded square for the ribcage and a triangle for the pelvis. Indicate the bones as shown.

2

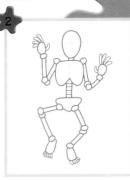

Draw the bones more fully, add shape to the ribcage and the spine.

3

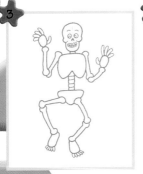

Add the facial features as shown here.

4

Add the bones of the ribcage and movement lines for that dancing look.

FRANKENSTEIN'S MONSTER

Here's a creepy creation for you to draw.

Lightly sketch in these simple shapes to begin with.

Add the shapes shown here for hands and the basic vest and jacket.

Draw the fingers and the neck and ankle bolts. Add a frayed look to the vest and jacket.

Draw the facial details. The brow is halfway down the face. Draw the hairline and a scar on his forehead. Don't forget the ears!

Add all the finishing touches: give a crumpled look to his clothes, a cropped haircut and metal studs on his chunky boots. Place him in the right setting – maybe an old-fashioned laboratory in a spooky castle. Outline the picture in pen, rub out pencil lines and colour it in.

CYCLOPS

Try drawing this one-eyed monster!

Sketch a circle for the head with an oval inside. Mark on a cross to help position the facial features. Draw in a big oval for the body and add shapes for arms, legs and feet.

Using the cross as a guide, draw in the face. Look at that beady eye! Next, add the hands and the tree trunk that he's holding.

3

Draw the clothes in more detail, adding crease lines. Put details on the tree trunk and draw two little skulls hanging down from his tunic.

Finish off with details such as his big, furry hat, bushy moustache and wart hog-type teeth! Give the tunic a woolly look and add hair to the back of his hand. Put your cyclops in a landscape of trees and distant hills. By making the trees small, he'll look even bigger.

WICKED WITCH

This witch will put a spell on you!

1

Draw the simple shapes shown here – don't forget the pointed hat!

2

Sketch in arm shapes and indicate hands and feet. Add a brim on the hat.

3

Draw a broom and a cloak for the old hag.

4

Using the cross as a guide, draw the details on the face: wicked raised eyebrows (show these by drawing a V), a big nose and chin, and a toothy grin.

Finish by adding warts on the nose and chin, and creases on the clothing. You might like to draw a bubbling cauldron ready for the witch to perform some hocus-pocus!

MUMMY'S HEAD

Beware of the curse of this mummy!

1

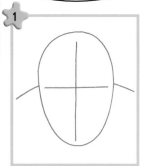

Draw a large, egg-shaped oval for the head. Add a cross.

2

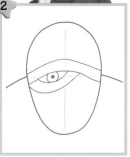

Using the cross as a guide, draw on one eye and two bandage strips.

3

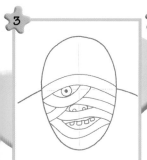

Add a bit of nose, mouth and teeth showing through, and fill in some more strips.

4

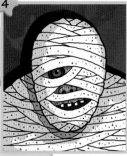

Lastly, draw the rest of the bandages. Add a few dots here and there and shade in the exposed areas beneath.

WALKING MUMMY

Take your mummy for a walk!

1

2

Sketch the simple, basic shapes as shown.

Using the shapes as a guide, define the body more clearly.

Cover him in lots of bandages and draw some movement lines to show him walking out of his mummy case. Add some trailing bandages.

VAMPIRE BAT

Draw this flying fiend.

Draw an oval for the head and egg shapes for the ears. Sketch the wings using a V shape as shown.

Draw the wing and claw shapes. Add the legs and detail to the ears.

Put finishing details on the wings and use the cross as a guide to draw in the face.

Give your bat a hairy body. Add movement lines. Outline the bat in pen and colour it in.

COUNT DRACULA

Draw this famous aristocratic vampire.

1

Draw ovals for the head and body. Sketch a collar, the bottom of the cloak and the feet.

2

Draw the crooked hand and add more shape to the cloak. Decorate the shoes.

3

Draw the face: a V-shaped hairline, a pointy ear, evil eyes and blood-sucking fangs.

4

Add the finishing details. A spooky castle looms in the background!